Two Little Witchlings series

The Day Death
Came To Visit

Written & Illustrated by
Becky Susan Adams

"As long as you hold someone in your heart,
you can never lose them. Ever."
~ Jack Frost (1998)

Dedicated to 'Bingo'

Rose Witchling knew something about today felt.. odd. The autumn sky was normal, and breakfast was normal, and the kiss on her forehead from Mama was normal. So why did something feel not-quite-normal?

After helping her Big Sister clear the table, Rose Witchling went to find Corbie, her pet Raven. He was a beautiful creature with jet-black feathers and strong, sharp claws, and he'd been her best friend for many years. When she got to his nest outside, Corbie greeted her with an excitable bounce and a throaty **GWAH!** noise.

Rose Witchling held out her hand (which was filled with blueberries) for him to see. He flew to her arm, and she stroked his warm, silky feathers as he pecked gently at the food. That's when she felt someone *watching* her. She looked around, and saw a little figure standing just a few feet away, head tilted, staring at her & Corbie.

"Who are you?" asked Rose Witchling.
"I am **Death**," said the figure.

Rose Witchling felt a shiver run down her spine. "Why are you here?"
"I'm here to help you understand me." Death responded.
Rose Witchling frowned. "You mean like why you make people die?"
Death tilted his head again, saying nothing.
"That's right, isn't it?" she pressed. "You take people away forever and make everyone feel sad for a long time. *Nothing* about you is good." She turned her back on him angrily.

"Most people feel that way about me," replied Death, quietly. "They hate me just for being who I am."

Rose Witchling felt a bit bad then. Sometimes she was treated differently just for being herself, and it didn't feel very nice.

She turned to look at Death curiously. "Someone told me that when we die, we turn into a bright star in the night sky." Death just gazed at her. "But I've also heard that we become ghosts and walk through walls, spooking people." Death chuckled a little. "And then there's the whole '*sitting in the clouds and having sparkly wings*' thing, too..." Death looked thoughtful. Rose Witchling felt frustrated.

"Aren't you going to *tell me* what happens when we die??" she asked.

"You've only told me what other people think. But I have yet to hear what you think," Death replied.

Rose Witchling was quiet for a moment. "I'm not sure," she said. "I don't really like to think about it. Dying is a sad thing."
"Dying can also be a **good** thing," replied Death. "Do you see that log over there?" he pointed to a fallen tree. "Years ago that tree was strong and tall. Then a big storm came and blew it down. Now it's dead."
"Yeah, and that's **sad**," said Rose Witchling.
"Is it?" asked Death. "Look closer. What do you see?"

Rose Witchling stared at the log. She saw mushrooms & moss growing on it. She saw woodlice & ladybugs wandering in & out of small gaps in the bark. She saw a line of ants marching along one of the branches. She saw a hole in the side that belonged to a family of mice.
"If that tree hadn't died, all those plants & creatures would have nowhere to live," said Death.

Hmmmm, Rose Witchling thought. I guess that's kind of okay.

"Dying can also be a **kind** thing," added Death.

"Okay, sometimes dying can be good, but it's *never* kind!" argued Rose Witchling, angrily.

"I recently visited a very, very old rabbit," replied Death. "His spirit was strong, but his body was weak. He was in a lot of pain every day, and had nobody to look after him. Eventually it became too painful for him to walk, or eat, or even breathe properly."

"So you made him die?" demanded Rose Witchling. "*That's so mean*!"

"Is it?" asked Death. "When I visited him as I am now visiting you, he greeted me like an old friend, and said he had been waiting for me. He no longer wanted to be lonely, or be in pain. He asked me to free his strong, young spirit from his weak, old body that once served him well but was now failing. Do you feel it would have been kinder of me to leave him to suffer just so he could be alive?"

Hmmmm, Rose Witchling thought. I guess not.

Death continued on; "Dying can also be a **necessary** thing."
"It is never necessary to make things die!" said Rose Witchling.

"I see you have berries there for your friend," Death replied, pointing at the blueberries in Rose Witchling's hand. "Where did they come from?"
"From our shrubs in the garden," she answered.
"How did those shrubs grow?" asked Death, his head tilted.
"With rain & sunlight & good soil," replied Rose Witchling, proudly.
"Good soil?" enquired Death.
"Yes, good soil," she repeated back to him. "My Sister says it's *full of nutrients and rich bacteria, which help things to grow & thrive*!"
"Where do those nutrients and good bacteria come from?" Death asked.
"Erm, well I- I'm not sure.." she said.

"They come from plants and flowers and trees," answered Death, "and sometimes other creatures. Things that have lived and died, and disintegrated, becoming part of the earth again, going back into the soil to grow new things."
"So without things dying and rotting away," said Rose Witchling, "we wouldn't have new things? Not flowers? Not even food?"
"That's right."

Hmmmm, Rose Witchling thought. I guess death can be necessary.

"What does dying *feel* like?" she asked.
"You already know what it feels like,"
Death replied. "Just remember what it felt
like before you were born. It's the same
thing."

Rose Witchling smiled. "Okay, but what
actually *happens*?"

Now it was Death's turn to smile. "You still
haven't told me what you think."
She thought long and hard. Finally she
said: "I think I will be surrounded by my
ancestors, and everyone I've ever loved. I
think it won't be scary, but rather
peaceful, like that feeling you get in a nice
warm bath... and I kinda like the idea that
my body will help new things grow," she
looked thoughtful, "I'd like to be a rose
bush. They're the prettiest."

Death continued to smile, but said
nothing. They sat together on a log and
watched the trees blow in the wind. There
was a pleasant silence.

Rose Witchling finally said what was playing on her mind: "Why are you *really* here?"

Death's smile faded. He looked over Rose Witchling's shoulder towards Corbie.
She then understood. "No! You can't take my Raven! He's my friend!" she cried.
"He *is* your friend, and you are *his*," said Death gently. "Which is why you will have noticed that he is not the same as he used to be."

Rose Witchling looked at Corbie, who was now sitting next to her. Death was right. His feathers were no longer black & glossy, but grey & fraying. His claws were no longer sharp & strong, but shaky & worn down.

Corbie was old, she realised. Very, very old.

She picked him up & held him close to her chest in a tender hug. Death reached out a hand & gently stroked Corbie's head.
Corbie closed his eyes and went very still. Rose Witchling noticed he wasn't breathing anymore. She hugged him tighter & looked up at Death.

Death smiled kindly, stood up, and faded away.

Mama dug a small hole at the end of the garden, and Lily Witchling found a beautiful handkerchief for them to wrap Corbie in. Rose Witchling placed him in the grave, and the three of them carefully filled the hole back in with dirt that Mama had mixed with seeds. Afterwards, they put a large, pretty rock on top to mark the space.

When it was all done, Rose Witchling's eyes were filled with tears. Even with everything she had discussed with Death, and everything Death had taught her, she still felt heartbroken to have lost her best friend.

"Mama?" she said. "Will I feel sad forever?"
"You will feel sad for a while, my love, "Mama answered. "But as time goes on, you will begin to remember Corbie with a smile instead of tears."
"I hope so," Rose Witchling replied. "This doesn't feel very nice at all."
"No, it doesn't," said Lily Witchling, putting her arm around her Little Sister. "But Corbie knew you loved him, and he loved you. *Nobody* can ever take that away, not even Death."

Rose Witchling sighed, and pulled Mama & her Big Sister in for a hug.

Rose Witchling chose the first morning that felt like Spring to visit Corbie's grave in the new year. She was still sad, but not as much, and she had begun to smile more & more when she thought of him.

She picked some blueberries, and went around the back of the house to the end of the garden. Spotting the pretty rock that they used as Corbie's headstone, she realised that all the seeds they had mixed in with the dirt when they buried him had begun to grow. There was a rainbow of wildflowers all over his resting place! It was absolutely beautiful.

The sun shone on Rose Witchling's face, and it felt like the Goddess herself was smiling at her.

Just then she heard a soft *gwah!* over her. Sitting on a branch above her head was a young raven, looking at her curiously. She stood up and held out a blueberry for him. He flew to her arm.

"My name is Rose," she said softly. "Would you like to be friends?"

The End ♥

talking about Death

TRICKY TOPICS WITH LITTLE HOOMANS

Sometimes hard conversations crop up without warning, or they come up naturally during already very emotionally difficult circumstances. Keep communications with your child open & kind, answering their questions as honestly as you can within the parameters of your beliefs, as well as other peoples. Here are some examples;

"Will my sad feelings go away?"
Sad feelings don't last forever. If you're reminded of the person who died, you may feel sad again for a while. People do feel happy again eventually, & it's okay if you laugh and have fun.

"Will I forget (person who died)?"
You'll never forget them. As time passes by you're likely to start feeling less upset than you do now and remember them with a smile.

"What will happen when *I* die?"
Some people believe that we return to the Goddess, others believe that we get to come back and try out a new life, fixing our past mistakes (and probably making new ones!). Many people believe it makes a difference if we are bad or good in this life, too. What do you think?

"Will I ever see (person who died) again?"
Some people believe that when we die, we move on to the spiritual world, kind of like ghosts, and are able to visit the people we love. Some believe our lost loved ones visit us in our dreams. What do you think?

"How old will I be when I die?"
You still have a lot of life ahead of you, so there's no need to worry. As long as you get lots of sleep & exercise, eat up your fruits & veggies, and drink lots of water, there's no reason for you not to live a long, long, healthy life!"

Acti ity Suggestions

Flowers grow in different seasons. As one plant dies, another begins to sprout! Can you design a pretty flower in honour of your special person? Don't forget to give it a name!

Sometimes we celebrate a person's life by doing something special, like throwing a party or visiting one of their favourite places. What would you do to celebrate your loved one?

Ask your grown up to help you draw a life cycle of a person. From a baby, to a toddler, to a child, to a teenager, to a grown up, and then an old person. Can you do this for an animal now?

Can you draw a portrait of the person that passed away? Use some paper & special photographs of them to help you. Perhaps draw them in their favourite clothes doing fun things!

Acti ity Suggestions

When we are sad, it can have physical effects. Ask someone to draw around you on a large piece of paper. Use it to draw how you're feeling in your body e.g. tired eyes, tummy ache, sad heart.

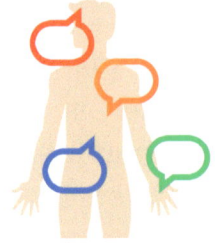

Rituals can help us remember people. Decorate a candle or carve runes into it, then light it at special times in the day or at night to honour your special person on their new journey.

On a paper plate, draw your face with the feelings you show to others. On the other side, draw your face with the feelings you keep inside/hidden. Talk about it with your grown up.

Make an area of Remembrance in your garden (if you don't have one use a window box). Include plants, flowers & features that your special person would have loved. Visit it often!

Activity Suggestions

IDEAS TO HELP YOUR CHILD PROCESS THEIR BEREAVEMENT IN PLAYFUL WAYS

Draw some hearts of different sizes. Can you draw or write what is inside your heart at the moment in each one? Include your feelings, worries, memories, hopes & dreams.

Collect a few things that remind you of your special person, or if you can't do that, draw them. It could be a book or some music, a snow globe or their favourite scarf, or some photographs!

Crying is super important. It helps us express sadness. Sometimes we cry alone, or with others. Can you make a list of your friends & family that you feel safe to cry to when you need it?

Sometimes when someone dies, they have a headstone at their grave with a message engraved on it. What would you write on your special person's memory stone? Put anything you like!

www.ingramcontent.com/pod-product-compliance
Lightning Source LLC
Chambersburg PA
CBHW041805040426
42448CB00001B/47